A Wor
of Clothing

Written by Janine Scott

macmillan
education

Ethiopia

Around the World

What is the weather like where you live?

Peru

Is it hot or cold?

Is it sometimes hot and sometimes cold?

Finland

Cold and Snowy

In some places, the weather is cold and snowy.

Canada

People wear coats
to keep warm.

Russia

People wear hats
to keep warm.

Alaska

People wear boots to
keep their feet warm and dry.

India

Hot

In some places,
the weather is hot.

Cuba

People wear light clothes
to keep cool.

Myanmar

People wear hats to keep cool.

Benin

People wear open shoes
to keep their feet cool.

England

Rainy

In some places,
the weather is rainy.

People wear raincoats
to keep dry.

Australia

People wear hats
to keep dry.

United States

People wear boots
to keep their feet dry.

After Reading

Let's Think About It

- What would you wear to play outside in winter?
- List all the things you would wear to keep yourself dry in rainy weather.
- What is your favourite type of weather? Why?

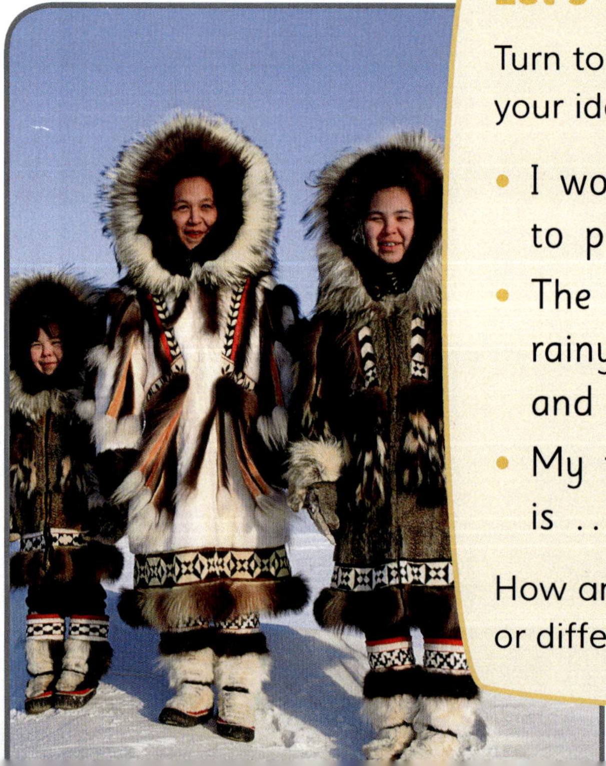

Let's Talk About It

Turn to your partner and discuss your ideas.

- I would wear ..., ... and ... to play outside in winter.
- The things I would wear in rainy weather are ..., ... and ...
- My favourite type of weather is ... because ...

How are your answers the same or different?